MW01079237

As a graphic designer who loves to color,
I am thrilled to combine my two passions
in the pages of my second coloring book.

Coloring allows me to explore my creative side
and experiment with all manner of materials
to create unique pieces of art.

I hope you create your latest
piece of art within the pages of my book.
I look forward to seeing all of your colored pages!
Post them on my website at
www.facebook.com/beckytorresdesigns.
Enjoy!

Note:
Markers and gel pens may
bleed through paper. Please
place a blank piece of paper
behind the page you are
coloring. Several are included
at the end of the book.

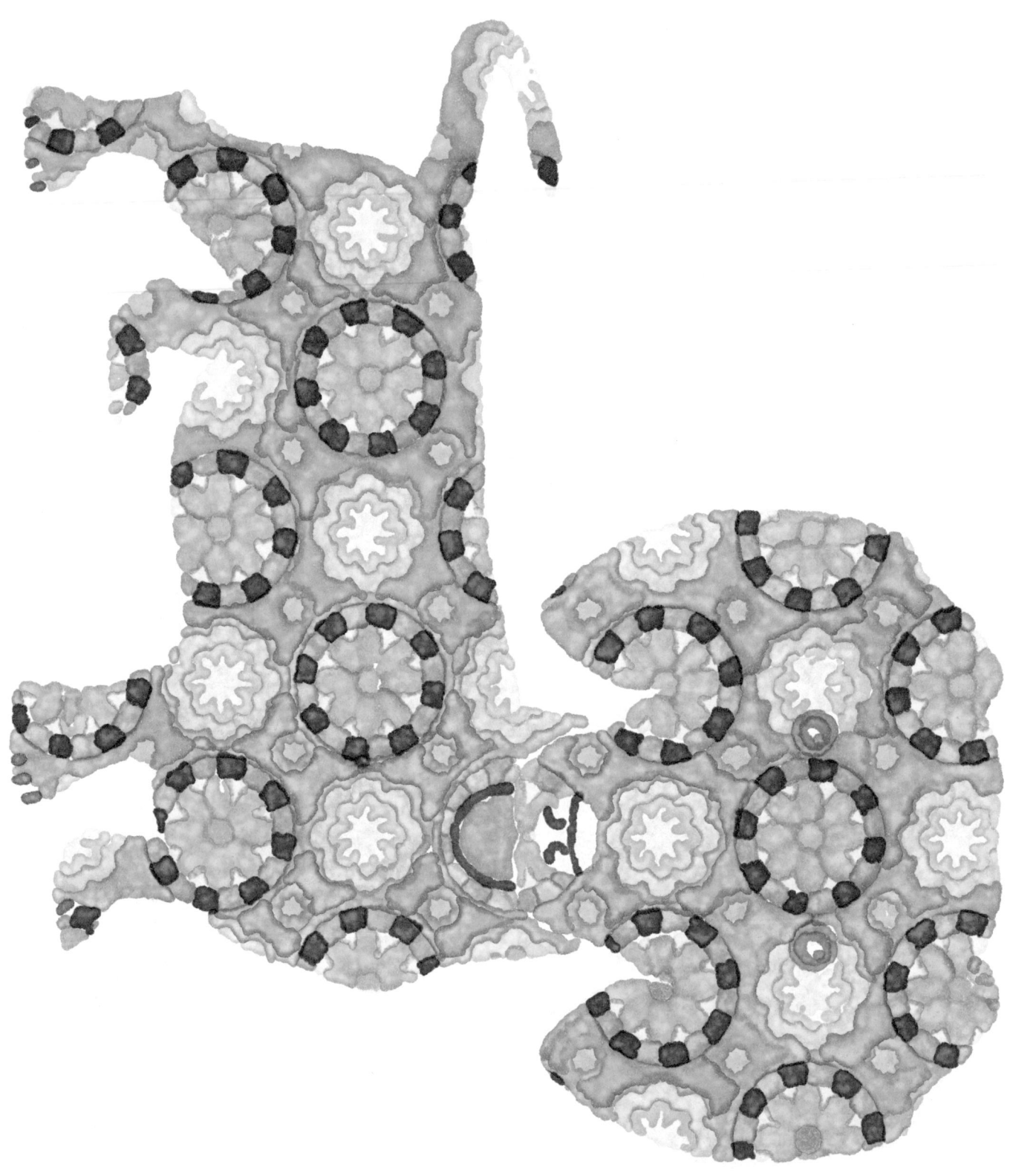